Original title:
Swaying to the Tropics

Copyright © 2025 Creative Arts Management OÜ
All rights reserved.

Author: Ryan Sterling
ISBN HARDBACK: 978-1-80581-670-6
ISBN PAPERBACK: 978-1-80581-197-8
ISBN EBOOK: 978-1-80581-670-6

Cascading Color and Light

Balloons drift by like jellyfish,
While parrots squawk a fishy wish.
The sun's a giant lemon drop,
That melts away with every hop.

With rainbow drinks that never spill,
And sandcastles that give a thrill.
Seashells dance beneath the glare,
Chasing crabs that don't seem to care.

Harmonies of Coral and Cobalt

A trumpetfish with shades so bold,
Stands in line for a drink, behold!
Clams play tunes beneath the tide,
As beach balls bounce and flip with pride.

Octopi in tuxedos sway,
Debating jokes about the bay.
With every wave, a giggle flies,
As fish wear hats of fruity pies.

When the Sea Breathes Kindness

The ocean grins with foamy waves,
Tickling toes of sunburned knaves.
Seashells giggle as they roll,
Holding tales of sandy souls.

Surfers riding on a snack,
With sandwiches packed in their pack.
The tides coax laughter from a whale,
Who narrates jokes with a big tail.

Palms Against the Sunset

Palm trees dance with a jovial sway,
Telling secrets of the day.
Coconuts drop with comical thuds,
Laughing as they land in the mud.

The horizon blushes, painted bright,
While tourists fumble their flip-flop flight.
Sunset piñatas burst with cheer,
Releasing riddles that we all hear.

Flavors of the Tropical Twilight

In the twilight, fruits do dance,
Mangoes giggle, take a chance.
Pineapples with their spiky hair,
Tell jokes that float upon the air.

Coconuts roll, trying to race,
While bananas wear a silly face.
A papaya twirls, slick and round,
As the moon begins to bound.

Strawberries laugh in a fruity cheer,
Making smoothies, never fear.
Cherries jump as if they're bold,
In this party of flavors untold.

Lemons toss confetti bright,
As the stars come out at night.
With laughter echoing down the shore,
Tropical fruits forevermore.

Shell Gatherings and Starry Skies

At the beach where shells do meet,
Crabs dance dance to a funny beat.
Starfish flip in silly delight,
Under the blanket of starry night.

Seashells gossip, oh what a crew,
Whispers of waves and tales anew.
A conch decides to tell a joke,
Makes the dolphins burst and poke.

The moon chuckles, casting light,
On sandcastles reaching great height.
With a wink, it plays a role,
Guiding sea creatures with heart and soul.

Gathering joys, we all comply,
Under the vast and twinkling sky.
In this shell party, laughter will flow,
As the tides dance with a giddy show.

Flavors of Fading Light

As the sun dips low with a giggle,
Cocktails mix with a playful wiggle.
Chill in the air, a dance of the breeze,
A pineapple hat? Oh, who can tease?

Laughter echoes, waves clap along,
Beneath a sky, where all go wrong.
Coconuts tumble, they bounce and roll,
Nature's comedy plays on, a stroll.

Mosaic of Paradise Lost

Bright colors splash; oh, what a sight!
Came a parrot that couldn't take flight.
He squawks in tune, with his feathers on fleek,
Grinning at folks with a playful cheek.

Crabs in a conga, they shimmy in line,
They stop for a snack, a feast divine.
With every pinch, they cheerfully shout,
While sunbathers fumble, in shades of doubt.

Driftwood Soul Serenade

Lone driftwood croons a sailor's lore,
With laughter, it sways, to the ocean's roar.
A conch shell giggles, plays hide and seek,
With laughter so loud, it makes dolphins freak.

The tide's a jester, waves ebb and flow,
Pulling in trinkets with marvelous glow.
Flip-flops dance like a dog on the go,
As sunsets whisper their secrets below.

Harmony in the Hummingbird's Flight

Tiny wings buzz like a caffeinated bee,
Dancing on nectar, oh joyous decree!
With flowers laughing, in colors so bright,
They swirl in a world, a sugary flight.

When branches jive, and the skies twirl round,
The hummingbird's laughter, a curious sound.
"Is that pollen or candy?!" it chirps with glee,
In their breezy ballet, oh, come feel the spree!

Vibrations of a Tropical Heart

Palm trees dance, a comical sight,
Coconuts falling, well, it's a fright!
Sunburned tourists in colorful gear,
Chasing the frisbee that vanished in beer.

Flip-flops flapping, laughter's our song,
Taking a dip, where the waves can't be wrong!
Ice cream melts faster than a fast track,
In this warm land, we've all lost our knack.

Sirens of the Saltwater Serenade

Waves whisper secrets, the fish know it all,
While seagulls squabble and bicker and squall.
Crabs in their dances, oh such silly prance,
Trust me, my friends, they'd give you a glance!

Sandcastles crumble, as dogs make their dash,
While moms sip their drinks, hoping to splash.
Beach balls are bouncing, oh what a scene,
Even the sunscreen is looking quite keen!

Dreamcatcher Under the Starfruit

Dreams caught in nets of a fruity delight,
Where mangoes giggle and stay up all night.
We've got piña coladas, the laughter flows free,
Slipping on banana peels, whee! Whee! Whee!

Night critters croon, in tropical cheer,
As chubby raccoons pull a party each year.
Under the moon, we dance on the sand,
All wrapped in coconuts, isn't life grand?

Radiance of the Coral Gardens

Coral reefs blush with colors so bright,
While fish in tuxedos put on quite a sight.
Octopuses waltzing, their style so bizarre,
Wishing on sea stars, wishing on a jar.

Jellyfish jiggle, in graceful ballet,
A comical sight as they sway and parlay.
With laughter and bubbles, we swim without care,
Enjoying the sea with warmth in the air.

Celestial Sea Foam

Bubbles dancing on the shore,
Laughing at the seagulls' roar.
Waves tickle toes, a playful prank,
While crabs in tiny suits do flank.

Sunburned faces, red as can be,
Clumsy dives, oh what a spree!
Flips and splashes, joy in the air,
Salted popcorn, without a care.

Sun hats flying, a goofy sight,
Ice cream melting, pure delight.
Mermaids giggle in the tide,
While fish drop beats with fins like pride.

Jellyfish jiggle, like silly fools,
Underwater dance, breaking the rules.
Coconuts laugh as they roll away,
In this frothy, fun-filled play.

Driftwood Tales

Driftwood logs tell stories grand,
Of pirate ships and treasure planned.
A crab in a hat, quite the star,
Argues with a passing jar.

Seashells whisper secrets old,
While starfish wear hats, bold yet cold.
Wooden planks with tales to share,
Of mermaids snagged in sun-kissed hair.

Flip-flops flop in a funny march,
Leading the way to the sandy arch.
Laughter echoes through the balmy night,
As shadow puppets take their flight.

Lobsters jive in clumsy cheer,
Moments like these, so sweet, so dear.
Tales of the tides, the moon's sweet grace,
In driftwood dreams, we find our place.

Jamming with the Island Breeze

Ukuleles play a silly tune,
Underneath a lazy moon.
Funky rhythms in coconut shells,
While parakeets sing, ringing bells.

A monkey dances, quite off beat,
Stealing mangoes, oh what a treat!
Breezy whispers in the palm trees,
Join the fun with a heart at ease.

Turtles groove without a care,
Flipping their shells in salty air.
Seagulls screech in comical fight,
As we all lose track of the night.

Pineapple hats on everyone's head,
While laughter rolls like waves instead.
Jams we make with our goofy crew,
Island life is the best, it's true!

The Sweet Surrender of Day

The sun dips down, a golden glob,
Painting the sky, a colorful blob.
Flip-flops fly as the day ends,
In this silly dance, we make amends.

Laughter echoes through the sand,
Seashells rolled as if by hand.
Starry wishes fill the night,
As fireflies join in on the light.

Corn on the cob, a tasty treat,
With sticky fingers, oh, such a feat!
Oh, the joy of messy smiles,
Chasing waves for carefree miles.

As night falls softly, dreams take flight,
With silly fancies, wild and bright.
The ocean hums its gentle tune,
Under the watch of the silly moon.

Song of the Emerald Coast

In flip-flops, I dance with flair,
While crabs stare back, with a dazed glare.
Seagulls squawk like they know the beat,
And beach balls bounce like they're on repeat.

The sun's a jester in bright disguise,
With shades on, I'm the wise guy.
Sandcastles crumble, oh what a sight,
As kids wage war in the midday light.

Hats blown off with a gust of breeze,
I chase them down with a sense of ease.
Life's a game in this sunny lair,
With laughter echoing everywhere.

So grab a drink, let's toast with cheer,
In this zany place, let's disappear!
The emerald coast is our playful stage,
Each wave a verse, we'll never age!

The Call of Crystal Waters

Oh, crystal blue, you've caught my eye,
I take a dip, but watch me fly!
A splash, a flail, it's quite the show,
I'm swimming like a fish, but moving slow.

The fish are judging, I feel their glares,
As I wave back with crazy flares.
Rubber ducks float by with style,
And dolphins giggle, it's quite worthwhile!

Lounging on rafts, I twist and turn,
With sunscreen slathered, it's my big concern.
A bird steals my snack, what a cheek!
Nature's comedy, so unique!

So let's embrace this water's call,
With belly flops and cannonballs!
In these crystal waves, we dive and glide,
Together in laughter, we'll forever ride!

Breathing in the Tropic's Essence

Inhaling scents of coconut bliss,
I dodge a bee with a clumsy twist.
The breeze brings laughter, oh what a jest,
A pineapple hat is my fashion quest.

Palm trees sway, they seem to giggle,
As I trip on roots and start to wiggle.
A parrot squawks, joins in the fray,
"Who's the comedian?" he seems to say.

Sunset parties, the rhythm alive,
Dancing with shadows, we all arrive.
With limbo contests so wildly fun,
It's a spectacle under the setting sun.

So grab your friends and let's just sway,
In this funny, sunny display.
Breathing in joy, the essence around,
In these moments, true happiness found!

Sunbeams on Silken Sands

Fingers in the sand, creating art,
A lizard joins in, full of heart.
With sunbeams shining, we play pretend,
Every grain tells a story, my friend.

My towel's a throne, I rule this space,
As waves invite me to join the race.
But oh dear! I stumble and fall,
"Majesty wipes out!" it's a funny recall.

Ice cream drips down in sticky trails,
Seagulls dive for my sweet details.
A sandman forms with a cheeky grin,
"Watch out for the tide!" he calls with a spin.

So let's bask in these golden rays,
With laughter echoing in warm arrays.
Sunbeams on sands, a riotous scene,
In this delightful dream, we all convene!

Tropical Fables in the Wind

In the jungle, monkeys dance,
They throw coconuts with sheer romance,
Parrots squawk a silly tune,
While iguanas nap beneath the moon.

A toucan wears a vibrant hat,
While chubby crabs play hide and chat,
Laughter echoes, bright and clear,
As fish wear sunglasses, full of cheer.

Palm trees giggle, swaying back,
While a lizard joins their wacky act,
The breeze, a playful friend at night,
Makes shadows twist in pure delight.

So grab your towel, take a seat,
In this fable, life's a treat,
Where laughter reigns and joy is found,
In the silly dance, we all are bound.

Serene Reflections on Ocean Blue

The ocean waves begin to brag,
A starfish sporting a jaunty flag,
Seagulls strut like they own the shore,
While crabs perform a tap dance encore.

Shells are gossiping like old friends,
While dolphins joke about their bends,
Sunbathers snooze and dream aloud,
Of catching fish that end up proud.

There's a turtle in a bathing suit,
Reading jokes on a beachy route,
With sandcastles filled with goofy grin,
Who knew the tide would let them win?

As sunsets paint the sky with glee,
The ocean's tales are wild and free,
In this blue, pure fun abounds,
With laughter echoing all around.

Blushing Skies and Tranquil Waters

Clouds puff up like fluffy pies,
As flamingos wear a bold disguise,
The sunset blushes, pink and bright,
While pirouetting fish steal the night.

A walrus plays the ukulele,
Singing tunes so bizarre and fray,
On lily pads, frogs cheer and croak,
As butterflies dance in a fine cloak.

In the hush of dimming light,
Laughter spills from left to right,
Stars peek out to join the jest,
While nature throws a lively fest.

In this place where silliness reigns,
And giggling ghosts run through the lanes,
Frolic and fun, a joyous quest,
Where every wave brings out our best.

Notes from the Tropic's Heart

In the hammock, a parrot jests,
While sunbathers nap, ignoring quests,
A breeze whispers tales of delight,
Keeping the island awake at night.

Coconuts giggle, row on row,
As tortoises make their fashion show,
Starfish debate who's the best dancer,
While the ocean waves keep the answer.

A flamingo grabs a quick snack,
And ducks make sure they're in the pack,
Jellyfish float with swirls of grace,
Making all the creatures feel their space.

So listen close to nature's hum,
Where laughter dances, bright and fun,
In this realm, wild and apart,
We'll forge the notes from the tropic's heart.

Lullabies of Lush Palms

In the shade, coconuts drop,
Laughter echoes, no time to stop.
Chasing crabs in sandy socks,
Time's forgotten among the rocks.

Mangoes flying, what a sight,
Everyone's dodging left and right.
The parrots squawk an off-key tune,
While limbo dancers swoon by noon.

A beach ball rolls, oh what a chase,
Someone lands right on their face!
With splashes loud and goofy grins,
The real fun here just begins.

Umbrellas tilt, drinks overflow,
Trip over feet, but that's the show.
In this paradise, oh so bright,
We're all just kids 'neath palm tree light.

Serenade of the Sunset Breeze

As the sun dips low, a golden gleam,
We toast to fish—oh, what a theme!
Hiccups blend with waves' soft sigh,
And seagulls dance as if they fly.

The sky's a canvas, colors clash,
Sipping drinks that make us thrash.
With fruity hats and laughter loud,
We serenade the evening crowd.

A twirl and shout, a friendly dive,
This laughter here keeps dreams alive.
Banana peels create a scene,
Where joy persists, and life's routine.

Under palm stars, off-key carols rise,
We mime like fish, oh what a surprise!
The waves just chuckle, join the spree,
In this funny, warm, sandy jubilee!

Rhythm of the Ocean's Embrace

Whirlpools dance, a splash and spin,
The ocean grins, let the chaos begin!
Flops and flails all dive with flair,
Splashing water everywhere!

With goofy strokes, we paddle wide,
Trying to surf, it's a bumpy ride.
Oh, watch that wave, it's closer now;
Sorry, but it takes a bow!

Salty snacks and critters roam,
Seashells whisper tales from a foam.
A dolphin jumps, we gasp in awe,
Then tumble down—oh perfect flaw!

The sea sings songs of silly woes,
Where jellyfish dance in flip-flop shows.
With every wave, we giggle more,
What fun awaits on this sandy shore!

Dance of the Painted Skies

Brushstrokes of colors, splashes bright,
We twirl in sandals, oh what a sight!
The sunset's waltz, a quick cha-cha,
While wind gives a tickle, 'Ha ha ha!'

Coconut hats with flowers abound,
Pirouetting on this merry ground.
With sandy toes and laughter loud,
We join the sky, oh so proud.

A misstep here, we tumble down,
Paint spills on the neighbor's crown.
But every slip's a part of the fun,
In this dance, we all are one.

As the stars come out, we spin anew,
With giggles shared, skies drift to blue.
In this tapestry, joy's the key,
Let's dance until we're wild and free!

Unraveling the Colors of Dusk

The sky spills orange like spilled juice,
Birds take off, forming a loose caboose.
Palm trees dance with a breeze so spry,
While I attempt to fly, but just sigh.

Flip-flops slap my feet in a race,
Caught in a game of tropical lace.
Coconuts roll like balls in the sand,
Laughter erupts—it's all so unplanned!

A sunburnt nose and a grin so wide,
As I chase a shadow, it rules the tide.
Sunsets drip like a melting treat,
While crabs are plotting to steal my seat!

The night descends, a mischievous grin,
Stars playing games, let the shenanigans begin.
In colors of dusk, life is a jest,
Tropical whimsy, we are truly blessed!

Emotions like Ocean Waves

A heart that ebbs, like a tide on show,
Joy leaps over like some wild marlin throw.
I trip on a beach ball, oh what a fall,
Laughing at seagulls who think they're so tall.

Ebbing and flowing, the laughter unfolds,
A beach ball adventure, we're breaking the molds.
Sandy surprises hide just out of sight,
Like the odd jellyfish planting a fright!

The waves tease my toes, then dash away,
With my best moves, I try to display.
But my flip-flops flee, like they want to race,
While I stumble along, dreaming of grace.

Bright colors clash in a sun-soaked spree,
As laughter ricochets, like fish in the sea.
Emotions buoyant, they rise and they dive,
Life in shades of silly, oh how we thrive!

Dreams on a Tropical Lullaby

In a hammock strung, life feels like a play,
Banana peels slip in a ridiculous way.
Crickets sing sweetly their night-time tune,
While the moon sneaks out to play with a balloon.

Coconut smiles as I attempt to sip,
Sipping spun sugar from a runaway trip.
Stars giggle softly, painting the skies,
While I twirl in dreams, just like fireflies.

Mangoes and laughter roll under the palm,
Sunshine and sweetness, a tropical balm.
As the night swirls, I give a loud cheer,
For dreams in this paradise cradle my fear.

Lullabies whisper, as I sway to the beat,
With visions of fruit, oh what a feat!
In every jolly note of the night, I find,
A carnival world that's both silly and kind!

The Heart of Water and Light

Hopping through puddles, a joyous delight,
Splashes like giggles, oh what a sight!
Reflecting the sun with every quick turn,
While sandcastles melt, as my spirits burn.

A sip of the sea, salt tickles my tongue,
Frogs croak a chorus, serenely unsung.
Water that dances like a playful breeze,
With laughter and bubbles swarming like bees.

The horizon blinks in a bright-eyed cheer,
As dolphins juggle with nothing to fear.
I trip over shadows, but who cares at night,
When every mishap becomes pure delight.

In the heart of this dance, water and rays,
We chase our laughter through light-hearted ways.
Amidst splashes and strokes, joy takes its flight,
In this merry-go-round of the day and the night!

When Waves Caress the Shore

The seagulls caw, a playful shout,
Their mischief makes the tourists pout.
As flip-flops fly, and children squeal,
A crab appears—oh, what a deal!

With every splash, the waves conspire,
To soak the beach with liquid fire.
A sunscreen battle, oh what a mess,
The laughter rises, who'll confess?

Ice cream cones dribble down my hand,
As kids build castles in the sand.
But wait, what's that? A sudden slip,
And boom! Down goes a vacation trip!

Yet through the waves and sandy blows,
We cherish each laugh that gently flows.
With joy that sparkles in the sun's embrace,
We dance on waves, oh what a race!

Tropic Reverie at Dusk

As day fades out and stars peek through,
A parrot squawks, what's he up to?
With coconuts tossed like dodging balls,
We giggle at fate as the moonlight calls.

The fireflies dance in silly chains,
While sea turtles join in silly games.
A sandcastle collapses in wild delight,
With beachside snacks taking flight at night.

The fishermen's tales grow wilder still,
They claim their catch caused quite a thrill.
But there's always a chance of funny blunder,
Like stepping in jellyfish—yikes! What a wonder!

So grab a drink and toast to flair,
As laughter bubbles in the salty air.
We'll twirl in skirts and wave our hands,
In this tropical dreamland of silly plans.

Interludes of Laughter and Light

The sun peeks out with a gleeful grin,
While beach balls bounce and begin to spin.
With flip-flops flapping, they join the chase,
Through laughter and giggles, we find our place.

A surfboard slides, oh what a sight,
The rider falls left, then right, a fight!
"A tide, a tide!" our friend just yells,
But the waves have secrets, oh who can tell?

A picnic blanket held down by breeze,
While ants march in like they're at ease.
They take our snacks without a care,
We chase them swiftly—how unfair!

The sun dips low, a fiery burst,
Our beach party's rules—just quench your thirst!
For in this hour, both day and night,
Funny moments linger, pure delight.

Festive Banter on the Beach

With bright umbrellas dotting the shore,
A toddler shouts, "I want more!"
As parents laugh, they take the bait,
Running after snacks, it's never too late.

The tide rolls in with a ticklish tease,
Tickling toes that quiver with ease.
A frisbee soars, but the wind has fun,
It veers and darts—oh, on the run!

Beneath palm trees, we gather 'round,
With jokes and stories in joyful sound.
The sea slaps back with a friendly cheer,
As laughter rises, our hearts draw near.

So join the fun, let worries flee,
Under sunlit skies, we'll be wild and free.
For tales and laughter shall truly flow,
On this festive beach where good vibes grow!

Lush Canopy Serenade

Bananaramas dance with glee,
Mangoes chuckle in the tree.
Parrots squawk in bright attire,
As coconuts roll in a tire.

Palm leaves wave like hands at play,
Coconuts echo, 'Hip hooray!'
Turtles trot with gentle flair,
In this sunlit, silly air.

Vibrant Vistas of Paradise

Colorful blooms make quite a scene,
Watch out for bees, they're all so keen!
Fruits look ripe, all ripe to prank,
As monkeys swing and laugh, we thank.

Picturesque skies with fluffy whites,
Seagulls glide in comical flights.
Flip-flops flop with every stride,
In this place where joy can't hide.

Gentle Tides and Tropical Dreams

Sandcastles rise, then tumble down,
Shells are treasures for the crown.
Waves come in, they dance and tease,
As crabs advance with silly ease.

Children giggle as they splash,
Bubbles pop with a bubbly crash.
Sun hats fly like boats on shore,
'Oops,' they say, 'We want some more!'

Fronds in the Sun

Under fronds with hats so grand,
Lizards sunbathe, bold and planned.
Frogs leap high with joyous cheer,
While turtles play at hide and seer.

Every giggle fills the air,
As fruit flies buzz without a care.
The breeze brings jokes from trees so tall,
In this island, we all stand tall.

Rhythms of a Sun-Drenched Day

The sun is a dancer, full of cheer,
With flips and spins, it'll bring you near.
A hammock's a stage, a pillow for dreams,
Where laughter erupts in joyful streams.

The waves clap hands to the beat of the sun,
As crabs do the cha-cha, oh what fun!
With coconut drinks and silly straws,
Who needs a plan? Just applause!

Birds in the trees, they sing off-key,
A concert of chaos, so wild and free.
Watch out for the mango, it drops from above,
It's all kinds of funny, but we still love.

So dance to the rhythm, let your troubles sway,
In this sun-drenched land, let's play all day.
With each goofy jig in the golden light,
Life's a big laugh under skies so bright.

Lullabies of the Lagoon

In a boat made of dreams, we float and drift,
With fish in a frenzy, it's a magical shift.
The frogs croak the notes, a serenade grand,
While turtles tune strings with shells in hand.

The breeze is a tickler, it blows with a tease,
As we giggle away, with such careless ease.
A splash from a dolphin, a cheeky delight,
Who knew the lagoon could be so bright?

Under palm trees that sway like a giggling child,
We share all our secrets, a bit wild.
With laughter like bubbles that rise to the air,
This lullaby's magic, beyond compare.

So sing with the waves, let your worries float,
Dance with the echoes, it's all quite a joke.
In the lull of the lagoon, we'll dream and we'll play,
Where life is a song, come join the ballet!

Wanderlust Under the Coconut Sky

With a map made of laughter, we wander about,
Through jungles of joy, there's never a doubt.
A coconut whispers, "Hey, have a drink!"
While squirrels throw parties on branches that wink.

The sun paints the ground, a bright patchwork quilt,
While seashells giggle, oh what a thrill!
In this land of the wacky, it's easy to see,
That life is a playground, come play with me!

A crab in a bowtie, he steals the show,
With moves so absurd, he's a pro.
Under coconut skies that sparkle and shine,
We'll dance like we're crazy, and drink fruity wine.

So let's pack our bags, leave worries behind,
With spirits so high, we're completely unlined.
In this world of whimsy, we'll laugh till we cry,
Chasing our dreams under the endless blue sky.

Hidden Pathways of Paradise

Down winding trails where the wild things play,
Are banana peels waiting to trip you today.
A squirrel on a skateboard zooms right past,
In this paradise, fun is built to last.

Tiny bugs with hats are hosting a ball,
While butterflies giggle, it's a grand free-for-all.
The trees tell stories with branches so wide,
As we wander through laughter, come join the ride!

In a pond filled with marshmallows, we splash around,
And crickets in tuxedos chirp their sweet sound.
Hiding from tickles of the soft summer breeze,
Nature's a comedian, if you just seize.

So let's chase the giggles, follow the light,
With joy in our hearts, we'll dance through the night.
In hidden pathways where laughter will grow,
Life is a treasure, come join the show!

Lanterns in the Night Lagoon

Glowing lights dance on the water,
While fish wear tiny, silly hats.
Crabs are having a lively debate,
About who fancied the best dancing spats.

A parrot squawks, 'Bring on the drink!'
A coconut floats, ripe for a sip.
As stars giggle above, so bright,
The night's a party, let's not skip!

Frogs in tuxedos leap with flair,
While turtles sway, oh what a sight!
The moon joins in, twirls with care,
As laughter echoes through the night.

Come join us here by the lagoon,
Where every critter knows how to groove.
With lanterns aglow, we sing a tune,
In this paradise, we all move!

Embrace of the Island Breeze

The palms are whispering secrets sweet,
While toucans crack jokes from high above.
Sandy toes wiggle in the heat,
As waves tease the shore with gentle love.

A beach ball bounces 'round with glee,
Chasing the dogs, who bark with joy.
Seashells giggle beneath the sea,
As crabs parade, oh what a ploy!

The breeze tickles noses, cool and spry,
As grass skirts shake in daring dance.
A lizard snoozes, dreaming high,
Of sunbathing with a glance.

When piña coladas start to flow,
And laughter bursts in rhymes and cheers,
We toss our cares to the frothy show,
With every breeze, we forget our fears!

Tidal Waltz at Dusk

As the sun dips low, the sea's a stage,
With jellyfish swirling, a grand ballet.
An octopus leads, turns with rage,
While starfish clap in a silent sway.

Sandcastles emerge, but soon they flop,
With each mighty wave that crashes down.
The tide makes a splash, a glorious pop,
Wearing shells like a glittering crown.

Dolphins giggle, splashing about,
Having contests, who leaps the most?
While seagulls circle, chattering out,
A wind-blown riddle of their coast.

As dusk paints the sky in pink and gold,
We twirl to the rhythm of the waves.
The beach is alive, stories unfold,
In this tidal waltz, everyone raves!

Carved in Sands of Serenity

Footprints trailing, but they won't last,
Like jokes told on the breeze, quick and light.
Sandcastles smile, but the tide is fast,
Turning laughter into a watery sight.

Seashells gossip, with stories to tell,
While flocks of seagulls steal the show.
A crab tiptoes, feeling quite swell,
Imitating folks who flow to and fro.

By sunset's glow, the horizon winks,
As the moon emerges all round and grand.
Awash in giggles and little clinks,
In this slice of bliss on the sand.

So build your castles, let laughter ring,
For every grain holds a moment's cheer.
In this haven, let your heart take wing,
And dance with the waves, without a fear!

Whispers Beneath the Coconut Canopy

Underneath the palm trees' sway,
Monkeys dance and steal your fray.
Coconuts drop, a surprise from above,
A coconut war? They must be in love!

Flip-flops flapping, the sun beats down,
Trying to dance, but I'll just frown.
A piña colada spills on my shoe,
Guess it's time for the splashes to ensue!

The breeze carries laughter, such a cheeky gust,
Who knew beach games could lead to such rust?
With every wave, my sun hat takes flight,
Chasing after it, what a silly sight!

The crabs join in with a shuffle and slide,
While I trip on my towel, with nowhere to hide.
Beneath the canopy where wild stories bloom,
We laugh until dusk, under the moon's soft swoon.

Echoes of Paradise

Bamboo flutes play tunes of the sun,
Seagulls squawk, oh what's the fun?
Jazzed-up fish splash in the bay,
To join this wild, aquatic ballet!

Flip-flop races along the shore,
Who knew footprints could hide so much more?
Sandcastles rise, then quickly fall,
The ocean's hangover? Just a playful call!

Laughter bubbles like soda on ice,
Every comedic slip just adds to the spice.
Chasing the breeze, what a glorious feat,
Two left feet, but I can't feel defeat!

In this echo chamber, the joy never ends,
With coconut drinks shared among friends.
Lively tunes collide in the air,
We're all laughable fools without a care!

Cascades of Coral Dreams

Diving down deep where colors bloom,
Coral critters dance, creating a room.
Sea turtles wink with a shell on their back,
Their underwater path, a wobbly track!

The jellyfish glow in a wobbly show,
As I try to surf on a wave that's too slow.
With fins a-flapping, I dash to the reef,
But a rogue wave sends me back in disbelief!

The starfish giggles, with a smile in sight,
While I tumble around, giving fish a fright.
Trying to swim with the rhythm of the tide,
Sinking down further, I can't find my pride!

In this coral dream, we all play the fool,
Each splash and giggle makes the ocean a pool.
So here's to the waves that carry us back,
To the surface where laughter begins to unwrap!

Heatwave Melodies

The sun beats down like a drummer in heat,
While my ice cream melts, oh what a feat!
Sticky fingers wave as we dance in the sand,
Catching our breath, it vanishes unmanned!

The beach ball's bouncing, a wobbly affair,
Just like my hair in this tropical glare.
Flip-flop flap, it lands with a boom,
Watch out for humor that fills every room!

Coconut cocktails mix with the sun,
Who knew being goofy could be so much fun?
A sprinkle of laughter and a splash of the sea,
Together we're light, like a jester's decree!

In this heatwave's song, we jive and thrive,
With every misstep, we come back alive.
So raise a toast to the sun's bright sway,
With smiles and giggles, we'll dance our day away!

The Dreamer's Cove

In a cove where dreams abide,
Laughter dances on the tide.
Seashells sing a silly song,
Even the fishes join along.

A crab with shades struts on the sand,
While seagulls weave a wobbly band.
Palm trees wave their leafy hands,
As sunburnt tourists build the stands.

Flip-flops flop as folks all prance,
Chasing seagulls in a dance.
Caught in nets of seaweed sweet,
The ocean whispers, "Take a seat!"

As sun sets low and shadows grow,
Mermaid jokes steal the show.
With giggles mixed in salty air,
The dreamer's cove, beyond compare.

Timeless Tides

At dawn, the ocean cracks a grin,
As jellyfish begin to spin.
Waves carry gossip from afar,
While surfers chase that golden star.

A dolphin shows off flips and tricks,
Telling tales of candy licks.
Clams snap their shells in pure delight,
In this laughter, all feels right.

Sunbathers fry like sunny eggs,
Meanwhile, crabs dance on their legs.
With ice cream cones that drip and drop,
No one here could ever stop.

As night arrives with stars in sight,
The ocean chuckles, deep and bright.
Timeless tides keep rolling on,
And every worry soon is gone.

Kaleidoscope of Coral

In waters clear, a dance unfolds,
Where colorful fish break all the molds.
A clownfish laughs with every flip,
While crabs join in a funky trip.

Starfish lounge in styles so grand,
With jellies swaying, pink and planned.
Manta rays glide with a twist,
They giggle as they dance and twist.

The sea anemones wave away,
"You gotta join this underwater play!"
With coral reefs all dressed in hues,
Every glance reveals a fresh muse.

As night descends and glowworms gleam,
This kaleidoscope becomes a dream.
With sea critters laughing all night long,
In this watery world, they all belong.

Valleys of Green and Gold

In valleys bright where sunsets bathe,
The trees wear crowns, and flowers rave.
Frogs wear tuxedos to the bash,
As lightning bugs light up in a flash.

Monkeys swing with playful glee,
While parrots sip their cups of tea.
Swirling breezes tease their tails,
As laughter echoes through the trails.

In puddles deep, the tadpoles leap,
While owls in hats start counting sheep.
Where pineapple pizza wins the prize,
And every bounce brings new surprise.

As stars peek out and fireflies play,
The valleys echo jokes of the day.
A silly world, bright and bold,
In valleys green and draped in gold.

Beneath the Banyan's Whisper

In the shadow of leaves, a dance starts,
A monkey throws coconuts, full of arts.
He wiggles his tail with such flair,
While a parrot sings gossip in midair.

Laughter erupts from the colorful crew,
As the locals join in, it's quite the view.
They slip on some peels while trying to feast,
Declaring a contest – who'll be the beast?

Under the branches, the party ignites,
With dancing and play, oh what delightful sights.
But the banyan just chuckles, swaying with glee,
Watching the chaos like it's a TV spree.

As sunset approaches, the joy won't cease,
The laughter grows louder, the spirit's at peace.
In the roots of the banyan, secrets do blend,
Where fun never stops and the silliness bends.

Secrets of the Seafoam Trail

Upon the shore where the sea laughs out loud,
Beachgoers trip over toes, feeling proud.
Waves toss their sandals, and smiles start to bloom,
As seagulls declare this a beachside room.

A crab in a hat wanders by with such flair,
Showing off moves, no one's quite aware.
Kids giggle and chase, their buckets in hand,
Collecting the treasures that wash up on land.

A jellyfish beams, it's soft like a cloud,
Surrounded by shouts that are sunny and loud.
But careful, dear friend, don't step on that goo,
Or find yourself dancing like a strange shoe!

As twilight descends, more laughter will rise,
There's magic in memories, beneath twilight skies.
With each splash and giggle, a tale starts to weave,
On the secrets that linger along the sea's sleeve.

Twilight Tales from the Faraway Shores

As the sun dips low, the stories commence,
Of pirates and treasures that make no sense.
A shark in a top hat, so dapper, so neat,
Is challenging sailors to a dance on their feet.

On a boat made of dreams, the crew's out of sight,
But the rum's flowing freely, oh what a night!
They tickle the octopus, making a fuss,
While dolphins join in, adding to the bus.

Beneath twinkling stars, the tales start to twine,
With laughter erupting over glasses of brine.
A mermaid giggles, her hair all askew,
As she joins the revelry, just for a view.

So pop on your eyepatch and sail on the breeze,
Where tales get spun under swaying palm trees.
With every wild whisper, each joke and each song,
At the faraway shores, where we all belong.

Essence of the Fallen Frangipani

Drops of perfume drift from blossoms laid low,
While humans delight in the scent, stealing a show.
They trip over petals, and tumble with glee,
Creating a dance floor where flowers agree.

A lizard in sunglasses lounges just right,
Claiming his throne as the king of the night.
When a breeze brings a tickle, how they all laugh,
As a dog joins the fun, taking a bow on behalf.

Each fragrance that wafts brings stories untold,
Of laughter and mishaps, of friends brave and bold.
A game of charades erupts on the grass,
As shadows do dance, and the moments all pass.

So gather around for the joy and the cheer,
In this fragrant escape, leave behind every fear.
For amidst fallen blooms, life's humor does shine,
Making memories sweet with the essence divine.

When Paradise Whispers

In a hammock made of dreams, I lie,
With coconuts adding to my pie.
A parrot squawks, sounding quite sweet,
While crabs compete, dancing on feet.

The breeze knows my secret snack plan,
As I munch on fruit like a big fan.
Palm trees grin with their leafy flair,
And I wonder if they have a pair.

The sun took a dive, but I'm still here,
With a bright pink drink, I have no fear.
Laughter echoes through the soft sand,
As waves tickle toes, oh so grand!

As day twirls night in a merry whirl,
A firefly sets off, giving a twirl.
In paradise, joy's the only law,
I giggle at life; it's quite the show.

Radiance of the Jungle Path

On a trail where shadows play tag,
I spot a monkey with a bright rag.
He gestures wildly, as if to say,
"Join the dance! Don't waste the day!"

Lianas twist like they're in a chair,
While toucans dive through sweet, warm air.
A snake's on break, taking a nap,
But here comes a frog, doing a tap.

Creepy crawlers in a funny parade,
A turtle's hat—yes, it's homemade!
The vines laugh softly, tickling my face,
As I trip on roots in this wild place.

With every step, there's a joyful cheer,
And a nearby buzz suggests a bee's here.
Nature's giggles dance in the sun,
What a silly show, oh what fun!

Chasing the Sunset's Embrace

As the sun dips low, what a glorious sight,
I chase it down with all my might.
A crab waves hello, snapping its claw,
While I stumble and giggle, oh what a faux pas.

The clouds are painted in shades so grand,
I trip on the shore, losing my stand.
Splashing in puddles, like a big kid,
The tide calls my name, oh, how could I hid?

A seagull steals fries right from my hand,
I shout, "Hey, buddy! That's not your brand!"
The laughter rolls in with the coming night,
As stars peek out, sparkling bright.

The sun winks down, a playful tease,
While I dance with waves, feeling the breeze.
In this race to twilight, I find my bliss,
Oh, evening, don't go, I'll surely miss!

The Glow of Coastal Nights

Under the stars, I set my scene,
With a glow from lanterns, all in between.
The tide whispers jokes, waves crash with glee,
As crickets make music just for me.

In the sand, I draw my name with flair,
A whale in the distance takes to the air.
A coconut falls with a thud and a bounce,
As laughter erupts—oh, what a pounce!

Bonfires flicker as friends gather 'round,
Marshmallows toast, though they fall on the ground.
A friend tells tales of mermaids and sharks,
While shadows dance close, leaving their marks.

The night rolls on, filled with jokes galore,
Crashing waves echo and laughter soars.
In this coastal haven, our spirits unite,
With every chuckle, the stars feel just right.

Chasing Shadows on Mango Streets

Underneath the mango tree,
Lime-green monkeys swing with glee.
They throw down fruit, a fruity fight,
While I dodge mangoes, left and right.

Children laugh and dance around,
Their feet barely touch the ground.
A game of tag starts on the run,
I seek the shade but find the sun.

The ice cream cart makes a sly retreat,
While we chase shades, oh what a feat!
The sticky juice stays on our chin,
And all at once the laugh begins.

As shadows blend and time escapes,
We end up lost amid the grapes.
With sunburned noses, we call it a day,
And nap beneath the mango sway.

A Tangle of Hibiscus and Time

Petals dance like tiny feet,
In blooms so bright we can't be beat.
A tangle here, a twisty vine,
Flirting with the sun like it's a sign.

Grandma's tales of love and sun,
Wrapped in stories, oh what fun!
Yet bees have plans that steal the show,
Chasing each flower, to and fro.

We try to catch a single bee,
But end up tangled—no one's free!
The hibiscus giggles in the breeze,
As we get lost with so much ease.

Time slips by like a fuzzy worm,
We laugh and dance, our faces warm.
A tangle here, a hole there,
In this garden we haven't a care.

Breeze-kissed Rhythms

The breeze whistles and starts to hum,
As palm trees strut, here comes the drum!
We twirl around in silly fits,
While sandals fly from our little bits.

With coconuts on our moving heads,
We dance with shadows, leap from beds.
The rhythm's strong, we lose our shoe,
And laugh until we can't see through.

The wooden pier begins to sway,
Seagulls screech, "You've gone astray!"
But waves just giggle, winking sly,
"Who needs to know? Just let it fly!"

As evening falls, the stars align,
We spin in circles, my friend and mine.
With breeze-kissed rhythms in full swing,
We gather smiles, let laughter sing.

Lantern Glow in the Mist

When lanterns glow in evening's mist,
We play a game that can't be missed.
Ghosts and giggles fill the air,
As shadows dance without a care.

The crickets join our nighttime song,
While we march on, proud and strong.
"Don't look back!" we shriek with glee,
Pretending ghosts are after me!

The bumpy road leads us astray,
As we trip over what's in our way.
A lantern swings, a giggle's born,
And we burst out like a fresh new dawn.

With lantern glow and silly grins,
This game of fright is where it begins.
In the misty night, pure delight,
We chase our fears till morning light.

Song of the Island's Spirit

In the sun's warm embrace, a coconut claps,
A dancing crab prances, with slick little taps.
The parrot squawks loudly, in colors so bright,
While the coconut drinks rum, just feeling alright.

Lizards in shades, they strut with a flair,
With sunglasses perched, stealing sun with a stare.
The fish tell tall tales, all swimmingly grand,
While surfing on waves, so goofy and planned.

A flip-flop parade, oh the guests were a sight,
As they lounged on the sand, from morning 'til night.
With giggles and hiccups, the jokes flew like kites,
As the island's spirit danced in their sights.

Midnight Inspirations from the Lagoon

Under a moonlit glow, the frogs held a ball,
With top hats and tails, they danced one and all.
Fishes had a swim-off, of choreo so slick,
While turtles judged harshly, with critiquing so quick.

The stars winked with laughter, lighting the scene,
As seaweed 'dressed up' in a fashion routine.
With giggly sea urchins, who rolled on the floor,
While octopuses juggled, creating a roar.

The tides chimed in softly, with whispers of glee,
As crabs served up snacks on a platter of sea.
With cocktails of sea foam and starfish delights,
A gala of mischief danced through the nights.

Island Whispers

A hammock was swinging, hung high in the trees,
With a monkey, quite charming, just swinging with ease.
It tossed coconuts, hoping for a laugh,
While sunbathers squealed, spilling joy from their half.

The breeze brought gossip from flowers nearby,
"Did you see that flip-flop? Oh me, oh my!"
Shells sporting capes cheered, "We're fashionably late!"
As seagulls made comments, "You just can't relate!"

With tiki torches glowing, the crickets chimed in,
While turtles took selfies, wearing hats with a grin.
It's a photo op paradise, all laughs and no fuss,
In this carnival life, there's never a bus!

Dancing Palms and Waves

The palms snapped their fingers, in rhythms so fine,
With waves doing limbo, a true beachy line.
The sun threw confetti, with rays oh so bold,
While beach balls bounced high, with stories retold.

The steamy limbo contest made everyone gawk,
While crabs did their best, with amazing sea-walk.
With piña colada dreams, everyone's afloat,
As seagulls yelled "Bingo!" from their lofty boat.

The sandcastles sighed, with smiles on their tops,
While flip-flops forgot all their worries and stops.
Oh, what a fiasco, the island declared,
With a chuckle and cheer, all burdens were shared.

Embracing the Warmth of Dusk

As sun sinks low, the shadows dance,
A coconut falls with a clumsy glance.
Flip-flops misplaced, lost on the sand,
I trip and laugh, this isn't so planned.

The drinks are strong, but the laughter's stronger,
Uncle Joe's jokes are getting quite longer.
Seagulls cackle, they steal my fry,
I'm just a fool, who forgot to fly.

Palm trees sway with a bold little grin,
The day says bye, let the night begin.
I wear a hat that's twice my size,
In this sunset glow, I'm quite the prize.

With every sip, my worries drift,
In this warm dusk, all spirits lift.
The stars appear, so bright and spry,
And here I am, just trying to fly.

Breeze-Kissed Memories

A gentle breeze ruffles my hair,
Like playful kids, with no time to spare.
A beach ball rolls and bumps my knee,
I giggle and chase it, quite foolishly.

The waves invite with a foamy cheer,
But honey, those sunscreen spots appeared!
I slip and slide, oh what a sight,
My laughter echoes into the night.

Crabs scuttle off with puzzled stares,
While I'm just trying to locate my flares.
A drink in hand, with an umbrella bright,
Dancing on sand, it just feels so right.

Memories made with each silly fall,
Dashing away from that bug-eyed gull.
Here in this moment, all worries flee,
With breeze-kissed laughter, we're all so free.

Moonlit Shores and Ocean Calls

The moon peeks out like a playful tease,
Along the shore, I feel such ease.
With every wave, my worries depart,
Waltzing on sand, it's a nutty art.

The ocean hums with a glimmer of fun,
While I trip on shells, excuse me, hon!
I spin 'round, arms wide as a kite,
Under the stars, I twirl with delight.

The mermaids giggle, and I join in,
Their laughter lingers like a soft din.
Fins and tails, what a ridiculous sight,
I wave my arms, trying to take flight.

With giggles echoing in the shimmering night,
I frolic and dance, feeling just right.
In this moonlit realm, chaos takes hold,
As I hug my pals, our stories unfold.

The Art of the Island

An island canvas painted so bright,
With colors that giggle in pure delight.
I try to paint, but my brush goes wonky,
My masterpiece looks utterly bonky.

With fruit kabobs as my snack-time muse,
I dance and trip, but refuse to lose.
The laughter spills like a tropical drink,
In this funny moment, we all sync.

My flip-flop flies, oh what a soar,
It lands on Tim, now he's our floor.
We groove to tunes from a distant bar,
With twinkling lights, we all are stars.

So here's to the island, where fun runs free,
With silly blunders, just you and me.
In this joyful mess, we find our art,
In every chuckle, we make our start.

The Dance of the Pelicans

Pelicans in fancy hats,
They dance and trip in silly spats.
With wobbly legs and flapping wings,
They surely think they're king of flings.

They shuffle left, then shuffle right,
Making splashes, quite a sight!
They prance around like they're in a show,
With fishy breath from to and fro.

Onlookers laugh and point with glee,
As pelicans sip their coconut tea.
Their funny antics steal the show,
While sipping drinks from straws below.

When the sun dips low, they take a bow,
The coastal crowd can't help but wow!
With laughter rolling like beachy tides,
These feathered fools take the prize of rides.

Secrets of the Hibiscus

Hibiscus blooms in flashy hues,
Whispering tales of tropical views.
With petals as soft as summer's song,
They giggle in gardens, where they belong.

One flower claims to hold a secret,
About a crab who's quite the misfit.
He dances sideways to entertain,
While petals sway in a sunny lane.

"Tell me more!" the sunflowers peek,
As bees buzz in, seeking a sneak.
But the hibiscus, with a squinty flick,
Sips nectar—now that's the trick!

In a floral gossip fest they thrive,
With tales that make the garden jive.
So next time you smell a sweet bouquet,
Remember blossoms love to play!

A Lantern in the Warm Glow

A lantern hangs on a palm tree tall,
With a flickering light that winks for all.
It tells stories of nights filled with cheer,
And giggles that echo through the year.

It flickers like a sleepy eyelid,
While crickets chirp, oh so much amid.
The shadows twist for a boisterous dance,
As the moon gives stars a merry glance.

Oysters in shells come out to play,
With their pearly wisdom on display.
They laugh at the lantern, bright and bold,
In warm glow, their fables unfold.

When darkness falls, the lantern beams,
As if it knows all our silly dreams.
So let it shine and guide your way,
In this nightly jamboree, let's sway!

Paintings of the Twilight Isle

On a canvas of sunset, colors swirl,
As seagulls dive and small fish twirl.
Brushstrokes giggle as shadows dance,
While crabs in tuxedos sway and prance.

A painter paints with laughter loud,
While coconut whispers, "I'm so proud!"
The sky wears pink and orange hair,
Painting is fun, the sun's a flair.

Each wave that crashes, a playful splash,
As laughter bounces like a wild bash.
The twilight isle, with its glowing art,
Makes every heart sing and skip a beat in part.

So gather your brushes and let's create,
A masterpiece filled with joy, never late.
In colors bright, let's roam and play,
On this enchanted isle, come what may!

A Symphony of Sand and Surf

In flip-flops we dance, feeling so spry,
While seagulls steal fries, oh my, oh my!
The sun's on our backs, a bright golden hue,
We squeal with delight, in waters so blue.

A crab in a hurry, he's quite the sly guy,
Pinching our toes as he scuttles on by.
With sandcastles built, that won't last the tide,
We laugh as they tumble—what a fun ride!

Beach balls are flying, they float like a dream,
Kids chasing shadows, or so it would seem.
Ice cream on faces, with laughter galore,
Each moment a treasure, we couldn't ask more.

As dusk starts to fall, we dance in the light,
With fire pits aglow, oh, what a sight!
Underneath all the stars, we sing silly songs,
In this sandy paradise, where laughter belongs.

Rustic Charm of the Shoreline

The surf shouts hello, a bubbly old friend,
Seagulls are cawing, but we won't pretend.
Shells scattered like stories, all washed on the sand,
A beach day together, oh, life is so grand.

With sun hats awry, we gather our loot,
A flip-flop's gone missing, and so is my shoe boot!
The cooler is empty, save one can of fizz,
While sunburns, we giggle—what bliss this is.

Tide rolls in softly, with giggles it sings,
Waves tickle our toes, oh the joy that it brings!
Flopping like fish, we splash in delight,
Living for laughter, from morning till night.

Then up pops a dolphin, oh what a surprise!
He flips, he splashes, right before our eyes.
With cans in our hands and jokes in the air,
We cheer for our pal; there's fun everywhere.

The Lure of Distant Horizons

Daydreaming of places where palm trees sway high,
While sipping sweet drinks, with umbrellas, oh my!
The sun's on our noses, the breeze gives a wink,
A hammock awaits, let's not even think.

Oh look at that toucan, with colors so bright,
He squawks a loud tune, what a funny sight!
With each passing wave, our worries all cease,
The ocean's a canvas, paint laughter with peace.

Seashells and treasures, we gather in glee,
While crabs play tag, how silly they be!
A flip and a splash, we splash like the fish,
In the warm ocean's hug, we dance and we swish.

As sunsets surround, with shades red and gold,
We share silly stories, both new and old.
A bonfire ignites, with stories galore,
In spaces like these, we've got laughter in store.

Tropical Echoes in the Night

Beneath the bright moon, with rhythms that sway,
We dance through the darkness, and forget about May.
With ukuleles strumming, all hearts feel so light,
Every chuckle and giggle, is pure delight.

The crickets are crooning a symphony small,
While we attempt limbo and just about fall.
A drink in our hands, with umbrellas so cute,
We giggle and stumble, isn't this a hoot?

With laughter like fireflies, twinkling the air,
Under stars far above, camaraderie rare.
The warmth of the night wraps us up in its glow,
As the waves join the chorus, it's quite the show.

A toast to the moments that spark joy and cheer,
With sand between toes, our worries unclear.
In this land of mirth, where the spirit feels right,
We sip, sway, and sing through this magical night.

The Heartbeat of the Sea

The fish have formed a conga line,
Swirling and twirling, oh, how divine!
A seagull tries to cut in with flair,
But lands on a crab, oh what a scare!

The crab waves a claw, all full of sass,
"Not here for your moves, just here for the grass!"
The waves giggle softly, splashing with glee,
While the shells hold secrets of who they could be!

A dolphin wearing sunglasses zooms by,
Chasing a beach ball, oh my, oh my!
He's got dance moves that would make you weep,
As the waves rise high, promising no sleep.

But under the sun, all chaos aligns,
As a sandcastle leans, its kingdom declines.
The ocean whispers, it's all just for fun,
The heartbeat of waves will never be done.

Sunlit Horizons

Under the sun, where shadows do play,
A turtle on rollerblades spins all day.
Flip-flops go flying, folks dash in shock,
While crabs in sunglasses just sit and mock.

The coconut bounces, a wild little game,
Laughter erupts as it calls for a name!
"I'll name you Fred!" a child makes a claim,
While lobsters dance, totally unashamed.

A parrot plays DJ, cranking up tunes,
As a trio of fish start to jam with balloons.
They wiggle and giggle, in rhythm they slide,
As goats on the coastline take a joyride.

The horizon is painted with giggles and cheer,
With each wave that rolls, brings the next round near.
So raise your drinks high, let's toast to this scene,
Where laughter and sunlight reign ever so keen!

Echoes of the Coastal Breeze

The breeze tells tales of a crab in a hat,
Who once was a prince but now is quite fat.
He struts on the shore, saying, "Look at me!",
While the seagulls snicker, so wild and free.

A tandem of surfers rides in with flair,
One tumbles and flips, the other just dares.
They wipe out together, a splashing duo,
Soon making a splash, calling it their show!

The starfish plays chess with a beach ball in tow,
While a clam tries to help, but just won't let go.
Each echo of laughter from folks on the sand,
Creates silly stories, so awkwardly grand.

As sunbeams converge on this whimsical scene,
The creatures all plot for the best ice cream!
The coastal breeze chuckles, oh what a tease,
With echoes of joy fluttering through the trees.

Where the Ocean Meets the Sky

The horizon winks, it's a playful sight,
With clouds wearing socks, feeling out of right.
A whale hums a tune, off-key and bold,
While dolphins join in, their laughter uncontrolled.

The sun slips and slides, a mischievous friend,
As seabirds play tag, with no need to pretend.
A crab tries to dance, but his timing is off,
He stumbles and tumbles; all parties scoff.

The driftwood stands guard, a wise old sage,
Watching the antics, laughing 'til rage.
He mumbles old tales of the days gone by,
Where fish wore tuxedos and laughed at the sky.

As foam frolics high, and beach balls collide,
The ocean and sky, in a dance, they abide.
It's a circus of fun where wild spirits fly,
So let every wave be a wink from the sky!

www.ingramcontent.com/pod-product-compliance
Lightning Source LLC
Chambersburg PA
CBHW072223070526
44585CB00015B/1464